This book was compiled by Daniel Melehi with the A.I assistance of Inventabot

<u>Dedication</u>

I hope this helps all of my wonderful readers achieve all their goals in their business. And I would like to thank my wonderful wife for all of her continued support in all my ventures.

May 7 2023

Contents

Introduction...4

    Overview of Bubble.io...4

    Why Bubble.io is a great platform for building businesses.....6

    Purpose of the book..7

What is Bubble.io?...9

    History and evolution of Bubble.io.........................9

    Features and capabilities of Bubble.io 11

    Comparison with other app development platforms...........12

Success Stories of Bubble.io 15

    Case studies of successful businesses built on Bubble.io......15

    Analysis of the key factors contributing to their success 17

    Lessons learned from these success stories........................19

Building a Business on Bubble.io 21

    Getting started with Bubble.io.............................21

    Best practices for building a successful business on Bubble.io
....24

    Tips for designing a user-friendly and scalable app 26

Marketing and Growth Strategies 28

    Overview of marketing and growth strategies for Bubble.io
businesses 28

    How to leverage social media and other online channels to
promote your app 31

    Tips for optimizing your app for search engines and
increasing user engagement 33

Funding and Monetization 35

    Overview of funding options for Bubble.io businesses........35

    Best practices for monetizing your app................................37

    Tips for increasing revenue and profitability 40

Challenges and Solutions..**42**

Common challenges faced by Bubble.io businesses 42

Strategies for overcoming these challenges 45

Case studies of businesses that successfully tackled these

challenges..47

Future of Bubble.io **49**

Emerging trends and innovations in app development 49

How Bubble.io is adapting to these changes 51

Predictions for the future of Bubble.io 53

Conclusion **55**

Recap of key takeaways 55

Final thoughts and recommendations 57

Call-to-action for readers to start building their own

Bubble.io businesses. 59

INTRODUCTION

Overview of Bubble.io

Overview of Bubble.io

Bubble.io is a powerful and innovative platform that allows users to create web applications without the need for coding expertise. The platform provides a robust set of tools and features that empower individuals and businesses to build custom applications that are tailored to their specific needs.

Bubble.io is designed to make the process of building web applications easy and accessible. Users can create their applications using a drag-and-drop interface that allows them to add and customize various elements such as text, images, buttons, forms, and more. The platform also provides a vast library of pre-built components that can be easily integrated into applications.

One of the key benefits of Bubble.io is its flexibility. The platform allows users to create a wide range of applications, from simple websites to complex web applications with multiple features and functionalities.

Users can choose from a variety of templates and themes to get started quickly or build their applications from scratch.

Another significant advantage of Bubble.io is its ability to integrate with other platforms and services. The platform allows users to connect to third-party services such as Stripe, PayPal, Google Maps, and more, making it easy to add additional functionality to their applications.

Bubble.io is also known for its excellent customer support. The platform offers extensive documentation, tutorials, and a vibrant community of developers and users who can provide assistance and guidance.

In summary, Bubble.io is an innovative platform that offers an accessible and flexible solution for building web applications. With its drag-and-drop interface, extensive library of pre-built components, and integration capabilities, Bubble.io is an excellent choice for individuals and businesses looking to create custom applications that meet their needs.

Why Bubble.io is a great platform for building businesses

Bubble.io is a great platform for building businesses because of its simplicity, flexibility, and power. With Bubble.io, anyone can build a fully functional web application without the need for extensive coding and programming knowledge. The platform offers a wide range of features and tools that make it easy to create custom web applications that meet the specific needs of a business.

One of the main advantages of Bubble.io is its visual programming interface, which allows users to create applications using drag-and-drop components. This makes it easy to build complex applications without the need for extensive coding knowledge. The platform also offers a wide range of pre-built templates and components, making it easy to get started quickly.

Another advantage of Bubble.io is its flexibility. The platform offers a wide range of customization options, allowing users to create applications that meet the specific needs of their business. This can include everything from custom workflows and data structures to custom user interfaces and branding.

Finally, Bubble.io is a powerful platform that can handle even the most complex applications. The platform offers robust database management tools, dynamic API integrations, and the ability to scale applications to meet the needs of growing businesses. This makes it a great choice for businesses of all sizes, from startups to established enterprises.

Overall, Bubble.io is a great platform for building businesses because of its simplicity, flexibility, and power. Whether you're looking to build a simple web application or a complex enterprise-level solution, Bubble.io has the tools and features you need to succeed. So why not give it a try today and start building better businesses with Bubble.io?

Purpose of the book

The purpose of this book is to provide readers with real-world success stories of businesses that have leveraged the power of Bubble.io to build innovative and effective solutions. Whether you are an entrepreneur looking to launch your own business, a business owner seeking to improve your existing operations, or a developer interested in learning more about the latest technologies, this book has something for everyone.

At its core, Building Better Business is about showcasing the incredible potential of Bubble.io as a platform for building custom solutions that meet the unique needs of a wide range of industries and businesses. Through a series of case studies and success stories, readers will gain a deep understanding of how Bubble.io can be used to solve complex business problems, streamline operations, and create new opportunities for growth.

Throughout the book, readers will be introduced to a diverse range of businesses and industries, including everything from healthcare and fintech to e-commerce and social networking. By learning about the real-world applications of Bubble.io in these different contexts, readers will be able to apply these insights to their own businesses and industries, regardless of their size or level of complexity.

Ultimately, the goal of Building Better Business is to inspire and empower readers to take advantage of the incredible potential of Bubble.io to build better businesses. By sharing the stories of real-world businesses that have succeeded with this innovative platform, this book aims to showcase the incredible potential of Bubble.io and provide practical guidance and insights to help readers achieve their own business goals. Whether you are a seasoned entrepreneur or just starting out, this book will help you take your business to the next level and achieve greater success in today's fast-paced digital landscape.

WHAT IS BUBBLE.IO?

History and evolution of Bubble.io

Bubble.io is a no-code platform that has gained immense popularity in recent years. This platform allows users to build web applications without any prior knowledge of coding. Bubble.io has evolved a lot since its inception, and has come a long way in becoming a reliable platform for creating web applications.

The history of Bubble.io dates back to 2012, when its founder Emmanuel Straschnov was trying to build a web application without any coding experience. He realized that there was no platform that could allow non-technical people to build web applications without coding. This is where the idea of Bubble.io was born. The platform was officially launched in 2015, and since then, it has been growing rapidly.

Bubble.io started as a simple platform with limited features, but it has evolved a lot since then. The platform has gone through several updates and upgrades to become what it is today. One of the major updates was the addition of a responsive design feature. This allowed users to build applications that could work on different devices, such as smartphones and tablets.

Another major update was the addition of a marketplace. The marketplace allows users to buy and sell plugins, templates, and other resources that can help them build better applications. This has made it easier for users to find the resources they need to build their applications.

Bubble.io has also become more user-friendly over the years. The platform has a drag-and-drop interface that makes it easy for users to create and design their applications. The platform also has a visual editor that allows users to see what their application will look like as they build it.

Overall, Bubble.io has come a long way since its inception. It has become a reliable platform for building web applications without coding. With its user-friendly interface and powerful features, it has become a popular choice for individuals, startups, and businesses of all sizes.

Features and capabilities of Bubble.io

Bubble.io is a no-code development platform that allows users to create web and mobile applications without the need for coding skills. The platform has a wide range of features and capabilities that make it an ideal tool for developers, entrepreneurs, and businesses looking to build custom applications.

One of the key features of Bubble.io is its drag-and-drop interface, which makes it easy to create and customize web and mobile applications. Users can choose from a variety of pre-built elements such as buttons, text boxes, and forms, or create their own custom elements. The platform also features a wide range of templates and themes that can be used to quickly create professional-looking applications.

Another key feature of Bubble.io is its powerful data management capabilities. The platform allows users to store and manage data in a variety of formats, including spreadsheets, databases, and API integrations. Users can also create complex data workflows and automate tasks using Bubble.io's built-in workflows and triggers.

Bubble.io also offers a range of design and styling tools that allow users to create visually appealing applications. The platform features a wide range of fonts, colors, and styling options that can be used to create unique and engaging user interfaces. Users can also create custom animations and transitions to add polish and sophistication to their applications.

One of the most impressive capabilities of Bubble.io is its ability to integrate with third-party services and APIs. The platform features a wide range of integrations with popular services such as Google Maps, Stripe, and Zapier, allowing users to create highly customized applications that meet their specific needs.

Overall, Bubble.io is a powerful and flexible development platform that offers a wide range of features and capabilities. Whether you are a developer, entrepreneur, or business owner, Bubble.io is an ideal tool for building custom web and mobile applications that can help you achieve your goals and grow your business.

Comparison with other app development platforms

When it comes to developing apps, there are plenty of platforms available in the market. However, every platform has its unique features, benefits, and drawbacks. In this chapter, we will compare Bubble.io with some of the other popular app development platforms available in the market.

1. AppSheet

AppSheet is a no-code app development platform that allows users to create mobile and web applications using a spreadsheet-like interface. Compared to Bubble.io, AppSheet offers limited design options, and the user interface is not as intuitive as Bubble.io. Moreover, Bubble.io offers a more extensive range of integrations with third-party tools.

2. Zoho Creator

Zoho Creator is another no-code app development platform that enables users to create custom applications for their business needs. While it offers a wide range of features, it lacks the flexibility and customization options available on Bubble.io. Additionally, Bubble.io offers better scalability and faster development times.

3. Airtable

Airtable is a cloud-based software that combines the features of a database with a spreadsheet. It allows users to create custom applications using pre-built templates or by creating their own custom workflows. However, Airtable is not as flexible as Bubble.io, and it lacks the advanced design and customization options available in Bubble.io.

4. Wix

Wix is a website builder that also offers users the ability to create mobile applications. However, it is limited in terms of customization options and features compared to Bubble.io. Bubble.io offers more advanced features, such as custom workflows, integrations with third-party tools, and the ability to create complex applications.

In conclusion, while there are many app development platforms available in the market, Bubble.io stands out for its advanced features, flexibility, and customization options. It enables users to create complex applications customized to their business needs and offers a wide range of integrations with third-party tools. By choosing Bubble.io, users can be assured of faster development times, better scalability, and more advanced design options.

SUCCESS STORIES OF BUBBLE.IO

Case studies of successful businesses built on Bubble.io

Bubble.io is a no-code platform that empowers individuals and businesses to create their own web and mobile applications without having to write a single line of code. Over the years, we have witnessed several businesses build their applications on Bubble.io and achieve tremendous success. In this chapter, we will be discussing some of the most notable success stories of businesses built on Bubble.io.

The first case study we will be looking at is the story of AirDev. Founded in 2015, AirDev is a no-code development agency that helps businesses build custom software applications using Bubble.io. The company has grown exponentially over the years, with a 300% increase in revenue within the first two years of operation. With over 150 clients and 650 projects completed, AirDev has become a trusted name in the no-code development space.

Another success story worth mentioning is that of Onfleet, a San Francisco-based startup that provides delivery management software to businesses. Onfleet built its platform on Bubble.io and has since raised over $14 million in funding. The company now serves over 2,000 customers, including big names like Sweetgreen and Imperfect Foods.

One more example of a successful business built on Bubble.io is that of Bubblin, a platform that allows users to create and share interactive web books. In just a few years, Bubblin has grown to become one of the most popular no-code platforms on the market, with over 50,000 users and 100,000 monthly readers.

These three businesses are just a few examples of the many success stories that have emerged from the Bubble.io community. They serve as a testament to the power and potential of no-code development, and how it can transform the way businesses operate and innovate.

In conclusion, Bubble.io has proven to be a game-changer in the world of no-code development. It has enabled businesses of all sizes and industries to create their own custom applications, without having to rely on traditional coding methods. The success stories of AirDev, Onfleet, and Bubblin are just a few examples of the many possibilities that Bubble.io offers to businesses and individuals alike. With its intuitive interface and wide range of features, Bubble.io is sure to continue revolutionizing the way we build and innovate in the digital age.

Analysis of the key factors contributing to their success

Bubble.io is an innovative platform that has changed the way businesses approach software development. The platform has helped several businesses to create real-world applications that have made them successful. In this subchapter, we will analyze the key factors contributing to the success of businesses that have used Bubble.io.

One of the critical factors contributing to the success of businesses that have used Bubble.io is its ease of use. The platform is user-friendly and requires no coding skills, making it accessible to everyone. This ease of use enables businesses to create applications quickly, which is critical in today's fast-paced business environment.

Another factor contributing to the success of businesses that have used Bubble.io is its flexibility. The platform allows businesses to customize their applications to meet their specific needs. This customization enables businesses to create applications that are unique and tailored to their business requirements.

The platform's scalability is also a key factor contributing to its success. Businesses can start small and scale their applications as their business grows. This scalability allows businesses to keep up with changing market trends and customer needs.

Bubble.io's community is also a key factor contributing to its success. The platform has a vibrant community of developers who share their knowledge and experience with other users. This community enables businesses to learn from each other and keep up with the latest trends in software development.

Another factor contributing to the success of businesses that have used Bubble.io is its cost-effectiveness. The platform is affordable, making it accessible to small and medium-sized businesses. This cost-effectiveness enables businesses to create applications that would have been beyond their reach using traditional software development methods.

In conclusion, the success of businesses that have used Bubble.io can be attributed to several factors, including its ease of use, flexibility, scalability, community, and cost-effectiveness. These factors have enabled businesses to create real-world applications that have made them successful. Aspiring entrepreneurs and businesses can learn from these success stories and harness the power of Bubble.io to achieve their business goals.

Lessons learned from these success stories

The success stories of businesses built on Bubble.io have taught us valuable lessons in entrepreneurship and innovation. Here are some of the most important takeaways from these inspiring stories:

1. Embrace the power of no-code tools: The businesses that have succeeded on Bubble.io have done so by taking advantage of the platform's no-code capabilities. By removing the need for coding skills, Bubble.io has democratized the process of building software applications. This means that anyone can create a functional app without needing to hire expensive developers or programmers. By embracing the power of no-code tools, businesses can save time and money while still delivering high-quality products.

2. Focus on solving a real-world problem: The most successful businesses built on Bubble.io have been those that have identified a real-world problem and created a solution that addresses it. By focusing on solving a specific pain point, businesses can create products that are in high demand and have a clear value proposition. This is especially important in today's crowded

marketplace, where consumers have countless options for every product or service.

3. Iterate and test constantly: Building a successful business is not a one-time event. It requires constant iteration and testing to refine the product and improve the user experience. The businesses that have succeeded on Bubble.io have done so by constantly iterating and testing their products, using feedback from users to make improvements and refine their offerings.

4. Prioritize user experience: In today's digital age, user experience is everything. The businesses that have succeeded on Bubble.io have done so by prioritizing the user experience and creating products that are intuitive, easy to use, and visually appealing. By focusing on the user experience, businesses can create loyal customers who will return to their products again and again.

5. Build a community: The most successful businesses built on Bubble.io have created a community of users and advocates who are passionate about their products. By building a community around their products, businesses can create a loyal following that will help spread the word and attract new customers. This can be done through social media, email marketing, and other forms of outreach.

By learning from the success stories of businesses built on Bubble.io, entrepreneurs and innovators can gain valuable insights into what it takes to build a successful business in today's digital age. From embracing no-code tools to prioritizing user experience, these lessons can be applied to any business looking to succeed in the competitive marketplace.

BUILDING A BUSINESS ON BUBBLE.IO

Getting started with Bubble.io

Getting started with Bubble.io

Bubble.io is a powerful and innovative platform that allows users to build web and mobile applications without having to write any code. This makes it an ideal tool for entrepreneurs, small business owners, and anyone looking to create a custom application quickly and easily.

If you're new to Bubble.io, getting started can seem a little daunting. However, with the right approach, you'll soon be up and running in no time. Here are some tips to help you get started with Bubble.io:

1. Start with the basics

Bubble.io has a lot of features, so it's easy to get overwhelmed. Start by learning the basics, such as how to create a new project, add elements to a page, and set up workflows. Once you have a good grasp of the fundamentals, you can start exploring more advanced features.

2. Use the templates

Bubble.io has a range of templates that you can use as a starting point for your application. These templates cover a variety of use cases, from e-commerce to social networking. Using a template can save you a lot of time and effort, as you won't have to build everything from scratch.

3. Join the community

Bubble.io has a thriving community of users who are always happy to help out. Joining the community is a great way to learn from others, get feedback on your projects, and stay up-to-date with the latest features and trends.

4. Take advantage of the resources

Bubble.io has a range of resources available to help you get started. These include video tutorials, documentation, and a knowledge base. Make sure you take advantage of these resources to help you learn how to use the platform effectively.

5. Practice, practice, practice

Like anything, the more you practice using Bubble.io, the better you'll get. Don't be afraid to experiment and try new things. The more you use the platform, the more comfortable you'll become with it.

In conclusion, getting started with Bubble.io doesn't have to be difficult. By following these tips and taking advantage of the platform's resources and community, you'll be well on your way to building your own custom applications in no time.

Best practices for building a successful business on Bubble.io

Bubble.io is an innovative platform that allows users to build web applications without the need for coding. This platform has become increasingly popular among entrepreneurs who want to build a successful business. If you're one of those entrepreneurs, you might be wondering what are the best practices for building a successful business on Bubble.io.

Here are some tips to help you get started:

1. Start with a clear idea of what you want to build

Before you start building your application on Bubble.io, make sure you have a clear idea of what you want to build. This will help you determine the features and functionalities that your application will need. You should also have a clear understanding of your target audience, their needs, and how your application will solve their problems.

2. Use pre-built templates and plugins

Bubble.io has a wide range of pre-built templates and plugins that can help speed up the development process. These templates and plugins can also help you add advanced features and functionalities to your application without having to write any code.

3. Keep it simple

One of the keys to building a successful business on Bubble.io is to keep things simple. Don't try to add too many features or functionalities to your application. Instead, focus on building a minimum viable product (MVP) that solves your target audience's problems.

4. Test your application

Once you've built your application, it's important to test it thoroughly to make sure it's working properly. You should also get feedback from your target audience to see if there are any areas that need improvement.

5. Continuously improve your application

Building a successful business on Bubble.io is an ongoing process. You should continuously improve your application based on feedback from your users and changes in the market. This will help you stay ahead of the competition and ensure your business's long-term success.

In conclusion, building a successful business on Bubble.io requires a clear understanding of your target audience's needs, a focus on simplicity, and a commitment to continuous improvement. By following these best practices, you can build a successful and profitable business on this innovative platform.

Tips for designing a user-friendly and scalable app

Designing a user-friendly and scalable app is crucial to the success of your business. A user-friendly app is easy to use, while a scalable app can handle an increasing number of users and data. Here are some tips for designing a user-friendly and scalable app.

1. Keep it simple

Simplicity is key when it comes to designing a user-friendly app. A simple app is easy to use and understand. Avoid cluttering your app with too many features or options that can confuse users. Focus on the core features that your users need and make sure they are easy to access.

2. Design for mobile first

More people are accessing the internet through mobile devices than ever before. Designing your app for mobile first ensures that it is optimized for the smaller screens of mobile devices. It also forces you to prioritize the most important features of your app.

3. Use intuitive navigation

Navigation is crucial to the user experience of your app. Use intuitive navigation that is easy to understand and use. Avoid using complex menus or navigation structures that can confuse users. Use clear labels and icons to guide users through your app.

4. Test your app

Testing your app is essential to ensuring that it is user-friendly and scalable. Test your app with real users to get feedback on usability and performance. Use this feedback to improve your app and make it more user-friendly.

5. Use scalable architecture

Scalability is important for apps that are expected to grow in usage and data. Use scalable architecture that can handle increasing numbers of users and data. This ensures that your app can continue to perform well even as it grows.

In conclusion, designing a user-friendly and scalable app is essential to the success of your business. Keep it simple, design for mobile first, use intuitive navigation, test your app, and use scalable architecture. By following these tips, you can create an app that is easy to use and can handle increasing numbers of users and data.

MARKETING AND GROWTH STRATEGIES

Overview of marketing and growth strategies for Bubble.io businesses

Overview of marketing and growth strategies for Bubble.io businesses

Building a successful Bubble.io business is not just about having a great idea and building a functional platform. It also involves finding the right marketing and growth strategies to attract and retain customers. This subchapter will provide an overview of some of the best marketing and growth strategies that Bubble.io businesses can use to achieve success.

1. Define your target audience: The first step to any successful marketing campaign is to identify your target audience. You need to understand the demographics, interests, and behaviors of your target audience so that you can create a personalized marketing campaign that resonates with them.

2. Develop a content marketing strategy: Content marketing is a great way to attract and engage your target audience. You can create valuable content such as blog posts, videos, and social media posts that provide information, insights, and solutions to your audience's problems.

3. Leverage social media: Social media platforms such as Facebook, Twitter, Instagram, and LinkedIn are powerful marketing tools that can help you reach a wider audience. You can use these platforms to promote your content, engage with your audience, and build relationships with potential customers.

4. Implement search engine optimization (SEO): SEO is the process of optimizing your website for search engines such as Google, Bing, and Yahoo. By implementing SEO best practices such as keyword research, on-page optimization, and link building, you can improve your website's visibility and attract more organic traffic.

5. Use paid advertising: Paid advertising is a great way to reach a targeted audience quickly. You can use platforms such as Google Ads, Facebook Ads, and LinkedIn Ads to create targeted ads that reach your ideal customers.

6. Build a referral program: Referral marketing is a powerful way to acquire new customers. By incentivizing your existing customers to refer their friends and family to your business, you can quickly expand your customer base and increase your revenue.

In conclusion, marketing and growth strategies are critical to the success of any Bubble.io business. By understanding your target audience, creating valuable content, leveraging social media, implementing SEO best practices, using paid advertising, and building a referral program, you can achieve success and grow your business.

How to leverage social media and other online channels to promote your app

In today's world, social media and other online channels have become a crucial part of any marketing strategy. The same goes for promoting an app. The app market is highly competitive, and leveraging social media and other online channels can give you a competitive edge.

Here are some tips on how to leverage social media and other online channels to promote your app:

1. Identify your target audience: Before promoting your app on social media and other online channels, you need to identify your target audience. Who are the people that are most likely to use your app? What are their interests and preferences? Knowing your target audience will help you create content that resonates with them.

2. Create a social media strategy: Once you know your target audience, you can create a social media strategy that includes the channels you will use, the content you

will create, and the frequency of your posts. Social media platforms like Facebook, Twitter, Instagram, and LinkedIn can help you reach a wider audience.

3. Use influencers: Influencers are people on social media who have a large following and can influence their followers' opinions. Collaborating with influencers can help you reach a wider audience and increase your app's visibility.

4. Run paid ads: Paid ads on social media platforms like Facebook, Instagram, and Twitter can help you reach your target audience and increase your app's visibility. You can target your ads based on demographics, interests, and behaviors.

5. Leverage app store optimization: App store optimization (ASO) is the process of optimizing your app's listing on the app store. Optimizing your app's title, description, and keywords can help it rank higher in the app store search results, making it easier for people to find and download it.

6. Use email marketing: Email marketing is a great way to reach out to your target audience and promote your app. You can use email to share updates about your app, offer promotions, and encourage people to download it.

In conclusion, leveraging social media and other online channels can help you promote your app and reach a wider audience. By identifying your target audience, creating a social media strategy, using influencers, running paid ads, leveraging app store optimization, and using email marketing, you can increase your app's visibility and ultimately drive downloads.

Tips for optimizing your app for search engines and increasing user engagement

One of the most important factors for success in the app world is visibility. After all, if no one can find your app, they won't be able to use it no matter how great it is. That's why optimizing your app for search engines is crucial if you want to increase user engagement and grow your user base.

Here are some tips for optimizing your app for search engines and increasing user engagement:

1. Choose the Right Keywords - Keywords are the foundation of search engine optimization. Choose keywords that are relevant to your app and the audience you're targeting. You can use tools like Google Keyword Planner to find keywords that are popular and have low competition.

2. Optimize Your App Store Listing - Your app store listing is the first thing users see when they search for your app. Make sure it's optimized with the right keywords, a compelling description, and eye-catching visuals.

3. Focus on User Engagement - Engagement is a key factor in search engine rankings. Make sure your app is easy to use, offers value to users, and encourages them to interact with it. This can include features like gamification, social sharing, and personalized recommendations.

4. Leverage Social Media - Social media is a great way to reach new users and increase engagement. Share your app on social media platforms like Facebook, Twitter, and Instagram, and encourage users to share it with their friends and followers.

5. Monitor and Analyze Your App's Performance - It's important to monitor and analyze your app's performance to see how it's doing in the app store and on search engines. Use tools like Google Analytics and App Annie to track user engagement, retention rates, and other key metrics.

By following these tips, you can optimize your app for search engines and increase user engagement, helping your app reach its full potential.

FUNDING AND MONETIZATION

Overview of funding options for Bubble.io businesses

Overview of funding options for Bubble.io businesses

As a Bubble.io business owner, one of the biggest challenges you will face is funding. Whether you are just starting out or looking to scale your business, you will need a significant amount of capital to achieve your goals. Fortunately, there are several funding options available for Bubble.io businesses. In this section, we will provide an overview of these options to help you make an informed decision about which one is right for your business.

Bootstrapping

Bootstrapping is the process of funding your business using your own resources, such as personal savings, credit cards, or loans from family and friends. This option is ideal for entrepreneurs who are just starting out and do not have access to external funding. While bootstrapping can be challenging, it allows you to maintain complete control over your business and avoid debt.

Crowdfunding

Crowdfunding is a popular funding option for Bubble.io businesses. It involves raising money from a large number of people through online platforms such as Kickstarter or Indiegogo. Crowdfunding is a great way to validate your business idea and build a community of supporters. However, it can be time-consuming and requires a significant amount of effort to run a successful campaign.

Angel investors

Angel investors are high net worth individuals who invest in early-stage businesses in exchange for equity. They can provide not only funding but also expertise and connections to help your business succeed. However, angel investors typically require a significant amount of equity and control over your business, so it's important to choose the right investor.

Venture capital

Venture capital is a form of financing provided by professional investors who invest in high-growth businesses with the potential for significant returns. Venture capital is typically used to scale a business quickly and can provide access to expertise and resources that can help you achieve your goals. However, venture capital comes with significant dilution and control, so it's important to carefully consider the terms before accepting funding.

Conclusion

Choosing the right funding option for your Bubble.io business can be a challenging task. Each option has its own advantages and disadvantages, and it's important to consider your business goals and financial situation before making a decision. Regardless of which funding option you choose, remember that building a successful business takes time, effort, and persistence. By staying focused on your goals and leveraging the right resources, you can achieve success with your Bubble.io business.

Best practices for monetizing your app

Best practices for monetizing your app

Creating an app can be an exciting venture, but it can also be challenging to monetize it effectively. With so many free apps available, it can be tough to stand out and make money from your creation. However, there are some best practices that you can follow to monetize your app successfully.

1. Determine your pricing model

Before you launch your app, you need to determine your pricing model. Will you offer it for free, charge a one-time fee, or offer in-app purchases or subscriptions? It's essential to consider your target audience and the value that your app provides to determine the best pricing model for your application.

2. Offer a free trial

If you're offering a subscription-based app, consider offering a free trial. A free trial allows users to try out your app before committing to a subscription, which may make them more likely to sign up. However, it's essential to provide enough value during the free trial to entice them to subscribe.

3. Use ads

In-app advertising can be a great way to monetize your app, but it's crucial to use it carefully. Too many ads can be annoying and drive users away, so it's essential to find a balance between ads and user experience. Consider using rewarded video ads, where users can earn rewards for watching ads, as they tend to be less intrusive.

4. Offer in-app purchases

In-app purchases can be a great way to monetize your app, provided they offer value to users. Consider offering additional features or content that users can purchase to enhance their app experience. It's essential to make sure that your in-app purchases don't feel like a paywall, and users can still enjoy the app without making a purchase.

5. Provide excellent user experience

Ultimately, the success of your app's monetization strategy will depend on the user experience. It's essential to focus on providing an excellent user experience and creating value for your users. If users love your app, they're more likely to stick around and even recommend it to others, which can help grow your user base and revenue.

In conclusion, monetizing your app can be a challenging process, but by following these best practices, you can increase your chances of success. Determine your pricing model, offer a free trial, use ads carefully, offer in-app purchases, and prioritize user experience to maximize your app's revenue potential.

Tips for increasing revenue and profitability

Tips for increasing revenue and profitability

Every business owner aims to increase their revenue and profitability. However, achieving this goal can be challenging, especially for startups and small businesses. In this chapter, we will provide you with some tips that can help you increase your revenue and profitability.

1. Focus on customer retention

Acquiring new customers is important, but retaining existing customers is more cost-effective. Focus on providing excellent customer service and building strong relationships with your customers. This will help you retain them and increase their lifetime value.

2. Upsell and cross-sell

Upselling and cross-selling are effective ways to increase revenue from existing customers. Offer complementary products or services that can enhance the value of their purchase. For example, if you sell software, you can offer training or implementation services.

3. Use data to make informed decisions

Data is a powerful tool that can help you make informed decisions. Analyze your sales data to identify your most profitable products or services, as well as your best-performing marketing channels. Use this information to optimize your marketing strategy and focus on what works.

4. Optimize your pricing strategy

Pricing is a crucial factor that can impact your revenue and profitability. Conduct market research to determine the optimal price point for your products or services. Consider different pricing models, such as subscription-based or usage-based pricing.

5. Reduce costs

Reducing costs can help you increase your profitability. Look for ways to streamline your operations and reduce your overhead expenses. Consider outsourcing non-core functions or automating repetitive tasks.

6. Expand your product or service offerings

Expanding your product or service offerings can help you reach new customers and increase revenue. Look for opportunities to diversify your offerings or enter new markets.

In conclusion, increasing revenue and profitability requires a combination of strategies and tactics. Focus on providing excellent customer service, use data to make informed decisions, optimize your pricing strategy, reduce costs, and expand your offerings. By implementing these tips, you can grow your business and achieve your goals.

CHALLENGES AND SOLUTIONS

Common challenges faced by Bubble.io businesses

As with any business or project, building a successful application on Bubble.io comes with its own set of challenges. Despite its user-friendly interface and drag-and-drop capabilities, there are still several common obstacles that businesses face when using this innovative platform. In this subchapter, we will explore some of the most pervasive issues that Bubble.io businesses encounter and offer actionable advice on how to overcome them.

One of the most significant challenges facing Bubble.io businesses is the platform's scalability. While Bubble.io is an excellent tool for small to medium-sized businesses, it can struggle to handle large-scale applications with thousands of users. This issue is particularly evident when it comes to data storage and processing. To overcome this challenge, businesses must carefully plan their application's architecture and make use of external data storage solutions like Amazon S3 or Google Cloud Storage.

Another challenge that Bubble.io businesses face is integration with third-party services. While Bubble.io has an impressive range of built-in integrations, it can sometimes struggle to connect with more niche or custom services. To overcome this challenge, businesses must be willing to invest in custom API development or seek out alternative solutions that offer similar functionality.

A third common challenge facing Bubble.io businesses is maintaining application speed and performance. As more features and data are added to an application, it can become sluggish and unresponsive, leading to a poor user experience. To overcome this challenge, businesses must carefully optimize their application's code and make use of caching and other performance-enhancing techniques.

Finally, Bubble.io businesses must also contend with the ongoing challenge of staying up-to-date with the platform's latest features and updates. As Bubble.io continues to evolve and expand, new features and functionality are added regularly, making it essential for businesses to stay informed and adapt their applications accordingly.

In conclusion, while Bubble.io offers a powerful and user-friendly platform for building applications, businesses must be prepared to overcome several common challenges. By carefully planning their application's architecture, investing in custom integrations, optimizing performance, and staying up-to-date with the platform's latest features, businesses can build successful and sustainable applications that meet the needs of their users.

Strategies for overcoming these challenges

Strategies for Overcoming These Challenges

Building a business is not an easy feat. There will always be challenges along the way, and it is important to know how to overcome them. In this subchapter, we will discuss some strategies for overcoming the challenges that come with building a business using Bubble.io.

1. Keep Learning

One of the biggest challenges of building a business on Bubble.io is the learning curve. The platform is easy to use, but it can take time to fully understand its capabilities. To overcome this challenge, it is important to keep learning. Take advantage of the resources available such as tutorials, forums, and webinars. Attend Bubble.io events and meet other users who can share their experiences and insights.

2. Focus on Your Goals

Another challenge when building a business is staying focused on your goals. It is easy to get sidetracked with new features and ideas, but it is important to stay true to your vision. Create a roadmap and prioritize your tasks based on your goals. This will help you stay on track and avoid distractions.

3. Test Your Ideas

Building a business on Bubble.io allows you to quickly test your ideas. Take advantage of this by testing different features and designs to see what works best. Use A/B testing to compare different versions of your app and gather feedback from your users. This will help you make informed decisions and improve your app over time.

4. Collaborate with Others

Building a business can be overwhelming, but you don't have to do it alone. Collaborate with other Bubble.io users to share ideas, resources, and experiences. Join online communities and attend local events to connect with other entrepreneurs. This will help you build a support network and learn from others who have faced similar challenges.

In conclusion, building a business on Bubble.io comes with its own set of challenges, but it is important to stay motivated and focused on your goals. Keep learning, test your ideas, collaborate with others, and stay true to your vision. With these strategies, you can overcome any challenge and build a successful business on Bubble.io.

Case studies of businesses that successfully tackled these challenges

In this subchapter, we will be discussing some real-life case studies of businesses that have successfully tackled the challenges of building better businesses using the Bubble.io platform. These stories will inspire and motivate you to take your business to the next level.

Case Study 1: Airtable

Airtable is a cloud-based software company that provides a spreadsheet-like database for users to organize and collaborate on data. They recently launched their new product, Airtable Blocks, which allows users to create custom apps using pre-built components.

Airtable used Bubble.io to build their Blocks platform, allowing them to quickly and easily create custom apps for their users. The platform's drag-and-drop interface made it easy for their team to build and test new ideas, allowing them to quickly iterate and improve their product.

Case Study 2: Squared Away

Squared Away is a startup that provides a platform for homeowners to manage their home maintenance tasks. They used Bubble.io to build their platform, which allows homeowners to schedule and track maintenance tasks, receive reminders, and connect with local service providers.

With Bubble.io, Squared Away was able to quickly build and test their platform, allowing them to launch their product quickly and efficiently. They were also able to easily add new features and make changes to their platform based on user feedback, making it a more user-friendly experience.

Case Study 3: Workstream

Workstream is a hiring platform for hourly workers in the hospitality and retail industries. They used Bubble.io to build their platform, which allows employers to post job openings, screen applicants, and schedule interviews.

With Bubble.io, Workstream was able to quickly build and test their platform, allowing them to launch their product quickly and efficiently. They were also able to easily add new features and make changes to their platform based on user feedback, making it a more user-friendly experience.

Conclusion

These businesses are just a few examples of the many success stories that have been built on the Bubble.io platform. By using this innovative platform, businesses can quickly and easily build better businesses, improving their overall success and profitability. Whether you are a startup or an established business, Bubble.io can help you achieve your goals and take your business to the next level.

FUTURE OF BUBBLE.IO

Emerging trends and innovations in app development

The world of app development is constantly evolving, and staying up-to-date with the latest trends and innovations is essential for any business or individual looking to create successful applications. In this subchapter, we will explore some of the emerging trends and innovations in app development, and how they can be leveraged to build better businesses.

One of the most significant trends in app development is the rise of low-code platforms like Bubble.io. These platforms allow developers to create powerful applications without needing to write extensive code, making app development more accessible to a wider range of individuals and businesses. Bubble.io has emerged as a leader in this space, offering a user-friendly visual interface that allows developers to drag-and-drop elements to create complex applications.

Another emerging trend in app development is the use of artificial intelligence (AI) and machine learning (ML). These technologies are being integrated into apps to provide more personalized experiences for users, as well as to automate tasks and improve efficiency. For example, AI-powered chatbots can provide customer support 24/7, while ML algorithms can analyze data to provide insights that drive business decisions.

Blockchain technology is another innovation that is starting to make its way into app development. Blockchain allows for secure, decentralized data storage and has the potential to revolutionize industries like finance, healthcare, and logistics. Apps that leverage blockchain technology can provide users with greater control over their data and enable new business models and revenue streams.

Finally, the trend of cross-platform app development is becoming increasingly popular. With so many different devices and operating systems in use today, businesses need to ensure that their apps are accessible to as many users as possible. Cross-platform development allows developers to create apps that work seamlessly across multiple platforms, reducing development time and costs.

In conclusion, staying current with emerging trends and innovations in app development is essential for building better businesses. Low-code platforms like Bubble.io, AI and ML, blockchain technology, and cross-platform development are just a few of the trends shaping the industry. By embracing these innovations, businesses can create more powerful, efficient, and user-friendly applications that drive growth and success.

How Bubble.io is adapting to these changes

As the world continues to move towards a more digital age, companies are being forced to adapt and change in order to stay relevant. One technology company that has been able to keep up with these changes is Bubble.io. Bubble.io is a no-code platform that allows users to create web applications without any coding knowledge. The company has been able to adapt to these changes by listening to their users and constantly improving their platform.

One of the ways that Bubble.io has adapted to these changes is by adding new features to their platform. The company has added features such as custom domains, SSL certificates, and e-commerce functionality. These features have made it easier for users to create professional-looking web applications. The company has also added integrations with popular services such as Zapier, allowing users to connect their applications to other services.

Another way that Bubble.io has adapted to these changes is by providing excellent customer support. The company has a dedicated team of support staff that is available to answer any questions or concerns that users may have. They also have a comprehensive knowledge base that provides users with answers to common questions.

Bubble.io has also adapted to changes in the market by offering a free plan. This plan allows users to create basic web applications without any cost. This has made it easier for small businesses and startups to get started with their web applications without worrying about the cost.

In conclusion, Bubble.io has been able to adapt to these changes by listening to their users, adding new features, providing excellent customer support, and offering a free plan. These changes have allowed the company to stay relevant in a rapidly changing market and continue to provide value to their users. If you are looking to create a web application, Bubble.io is definitely a platform worth considering.

Predictions for the future of Bubble.io

Predictions for the future of Bubble.io

As Bubble.io continues to gain traction in the tech industry, there are several predictions about its future that are worth considering. Here are some potential scenarios that could play out in the coming years:

1. Increased adoption by non-technical users: One of the biggest advantages of Bubble.io is its ease of use. With its drag-and-drop interface and visual design tools, even those without a background in coding can create complex applications. As more people become aware of this platform, we can expect to see an influx of non-technical users trying their hand at building their own apps.

2. Expansion of integrations: Bubble.io already offers a wide range of integrations with popular tools like Zapier, Stripe, and Google Maps. However, as the platform grows, we can expect to see even more integrations added. This will make it easier for users to connect their Bubble.io apps with other tools they use in their business.

3. Increased focus on mobile: While Bubble.io already supports mobile responsiveness, there is still room for improvement in terms of optimizing for mobile devices. As more people use mobile devices as their primary means of accessing the internet, Bubble.io will need to adapt accordingly.

4. More pre-built templates: Bubble.io already has a library of pre-built templates that users can customize to their needs. However, we can expect to see even more templates added in the future. This will make it easier for users to get started with their app development and reduce the amount of time spent on initial setup.

5. Continued growth of the Bubble.io community: The Bubble.io community already includes thousands of users who share tips and advice on building better apps. As more people join the platform, we can expect to see this community continue to grow and become an even more valuable resource for those looking to build successful apps.

Overall, the future looks bright for Bubble.io. With its intuitive interface, extensive feature set, and growing community, it is poised to become one of the leading app development platforms in the years to come.

CONCLUSION

Recap of key takeaways

Recap of Key Takeaways

If you have been following along with the success stories in "Building Better Business: Learn from Bubble.io Success Stories," you are probably curious about how to implement the key takeaways to your business. Whether you are a seasoned entrepreneur or just starting, the following recap will help you apply the insights from these real-world applications built on the innovative Bubble.io platform.

1. Identify Your Target Market

One of the most critical takeaways from the success stories is the importance of identifying your target market. This involves understanding your customer's pain points, needs, and preferences. Once you have a clear understanding of your target market, you can tailor your product or service to meet their specific needs. This will also help you to create more effective marketing strategies that resonate with your audience.

2. Focus on User Experience

Another important takeaway is the emphasis on user experience. In today's digital age, customers expect a seamless experience when interacting with a website or app. This means that you need to focus on creating an intuitive interface that is easy to navigate and visually appealing. Additionally, you should prioritize loading speed and make sure your website or app is mobile-friendly.

3. Use Automation to Streamline Your Processes

Automation is a powerful tool that can help you streamline your business processes and save time. By automating repetitive tasks, you can free up more time to focus on higher-value activities. Some of the most common areas where automation can be useful include marketing, customer service, and data analysis.

4. Leverage the Power of Data

Finally, the success stories highlight the importance of leveraging the power of data. Data analytics can provide valuable insights into customer behavior, market trends, and other key metrics that can help you make informed decisions. By collecting and analyzing data, you can identify areas for improvement and optimize your business operations for better results.

In conclusion, the success stories in "Building Better Business: Learn from Bubble.io Success Stories" provide valuable insights into how to build a successful business. By applying the key takeaways, you can identify your target market, focus on user experience, streamline your processes, and leverage the power of data to drive growth and profitability. Whether you are just starting or looking to take your business to the next level, these lessons can help you achieve your goals.

Final thoughts and recommendations

Final Thoughts and Recommendations

As we come to the end of this book, we hope that you have gained valuable insights into the world of Bubble.io and the amazing success stories of businesses that have leveraged this innovative platform to build their applications. We have shared inspiring stories of how entrepreneurs have transformed their ideas into reality and built successful businesses with the help of Bubble.io.

For everyone who is interested in building a business or application, Bubble.io is an excellent platform to consider. It offers a user-friendly interface and a range of features that can help you bring your ideas to life. You don't need to have any coding experience to start building on Bubble.io, and you can create a wide range of applications, including marketplaces, social networks, e-commerce stores, and more.

One of the key takeaways from this book is the importance of finding the right problem to solve. Before you start building your application, it is crucial to identify a problem that you are passionate about solving. This will help you stay motivated and committed to your project, even when you face challenges along the way.

Another important lesson is the value of user feedback. As you build your application, it is essential to regularly gather feedback from your users and use it to improve your product. This can help you create a better user experience and increase customer satisfaction.

Finally, we recommend that you continue to learn and grow as a business owner and developer. There are numerous resources available to help you improve your skills and stay up-to-date with the latest trends and technologies. Attend conferences, read blogs, and connect with other entrepreneurs and developers to stay informed and inspired.

In conclusion, we hope that this book has provided you with valuable insights into the world of Bubble.io and the amazing success stories of businesses that have leveraged this platform to build their applications. We wish you the best of luck as you embark on your own journey to building a better business.

Call-to-action for readers to start building their own Bubble.io businesses.

Are you tired of working for someone else and want to start building your own business? Look no further than Bubble.io. This platform has already helped thousands of entrepreneurs bring their ideas to life and turn them into successful businesses. And now, it's your turn to join the ranks of these success stories.

So, what are you waiting for? Follow these steps to start building your own Bubble.io business today.

Step 1: Identify Your Idea

Every successful business starts with a great idea. Take some time to brainstorm and come up with a concept that excites you. It could be anything from a new app to a subscription-based service.

Step 2: Research Your Market

Once you have an idea, you need to research your market. Is there a demand for your product or service? Who are your competitors? What makes your idea unique? Answering these questions will help you refine your idea and ensure that there is a market for it.

Step 3: Sign Up for Bubble.io

Now that you have a solid idea and have researched your market, it's time to sign up for Bubble.io. This platform makes it easy to build web and mobile apps without any coding experience. Plus, they offer a variety of templates and tools to get you started.

Step 4: Start Building

With Bubble.io, you can start building your app right away. Use their drag-and-drop editor to design your user interface and add functionality with pre-built plugins. Don't worry if you get stuck or need help – Bubble.io has a thriving community of users who are always willing to lend a hand.

Step 5: Launch and Grow

Once your app is built, it's time to launch and start growing your business. Use social media, digital advertising, and other marketing tactics to reach your target audience. And don't forget to continue improving your app based on user feedback.

In conclusion, building your own business on Bubble.io is easier than you think. With a great idea, research, and the right tools, you can turn your dream into a reality. So, what are you waiting for? Start building your Bubble.io business today!

www.ingramcontent.com/pod-product-compliance
Lightning Source LLC
Chambersburg PA
CBHW070837220526
45466CB00002B/805

9 7 9 8 3 9 4 1 7 6 4 2 5